ICO INVESTING

Complete Beginners' Guide To Investing In ICO's

Matthew Adams

Copyright © 2018 Matthew Adams

It is not legal to reproduce, duplicate, or transmit any part of this document in either electronic means or in printed format. Recording of this publication is strictly prohibited.

ISBN: 1987549759
ISBN-13: 9781987549751

CONTENTS

Introduction i

Chapter One: Introduction To ICO's 1

Chapter Two: Advantages And Disadvantages Of Investing In ICO's 16

Chapter Three: The Fundamental Factors That Affect The Value of A Cryptocurrency 23

Chapter Four: How To Choose The Right ICO To Invest In ... 30

Chapter Five: How To Evaluate An ICO's White Paper 48

Chapter Six: How To Evaluate The ICO Team 54

Chapter Seven: Evaluating An ICO's Market Projections And Competitor Analysis 61

Chapter Eight: How To Participate In ICO's 67

Chapter Nine: Best Strategies To Make A Fortune On ICO's 76

Chapter Ten: How To Avoid Getting Scammed 85

Chapter Eleven: Legal Aspects of ICO's 94

Chapter Twelve: Where To Keep Track of ICO's 100

Final Words 107

Introduction

Congratulations on purchasing this book.

In the last few years, cryptocurrencies have taken the world by storm, bringing with them a new way of doing things. They have also brought about new investment opportunities known as ICO's. Perhaps you have read stories about people who turned into overnight millionaires by investing in ICO's, and you also want a piece of this lucrative pie.

While they are certainly lucrative, getting into ICO's is complicated and confusing. Cryptocurrencies and the blockchain technology on which they are built are still in their infancy stages, which makes them complex even for tech savvy people. Additionally, ICO's are volatile and unregulated, therefore there is the risk of losing all your money. Where do you start? How do you know which ones to invest in? How do you avoid getting scammed?

The secret to navigating these murky waters of ICO's is to let someone who knows the way hold your hand. I have been involved in the cryptocurrency space since its start and I have invested and made a fortune through ICO's. In this book, I am going to share all the secrets I have learned from all the years spent investing in the crypto markets. I will hold your hand and teach you everything you need to know about ICO's. I will teach you what ICO's are and how they came to be, how to evaluate different ICO's and pick the right ones and how to identify and avoid scams. I will also give you the strategies that I have used to make a fortune through ICO's.

By the time you are through with this book, you will know quite a lot about ICO's, and you will be ready to step out into the market and start making yourself some money. Are you ready? Let's dive in..

Chapter One: Introduction To ICO's

In this chapter, you are going to learn about ICO, what they are, how they came to be, how they work, the characteristics of ICO's, the differences between ICO's and IPO's and the different types of ICO's.

Initial Coin Offerings (ICO's) have been attracting a lot of attention in the recent past. The attention has not been without good reason. In October 2017, a new software project known as Filecoin raised over $257 million in what is the biggest ICO so far. The guys behind Filecoin were not selling shares in a company. They did not even raise the money through crowd funding platforms like Kickstarter. Instead, they simply asked people to contribute funds to an idea in a new funding model that is taking the world by storm. Filecoin is not alone. In July 2017, another project, known as Tezos, raised $232 million in similar fashion. Many other projects have raised millions of dollars in a matter of days or weeks by issuing ICO'S.

By the end of 2017, ICO's had raised a staggering total dollar amount of over $4 billion. This is more than a 40-fold increase from 2016, when ICO's raised a paltry $100 million. This rapid growth of the ICO market and the explosion of the total market cap of all cryptocurrencies to over $400 billion is the reason behind all the attention ICO's are attracting. So, what are these ICO's and where did they originate?

Background of ICO's

Before the rise of cryptocurrencies, there were only a handful of ways for tech companies and startups with revolutionary ideas to raise funds. They could raise the funds by approaching venture capitalists and angel investors. However, this meant that they had to give away a share of their equity in the company to these investors. Alternatively, they could get bank loans or raise the funds through crowd funding platforms like Kickstarter. Similarly, small investors did not have much of an opportunity to invest in such companies. To become an investor, you had to have millions of dollars, know the right people and become accredited.

For companies that wanted to raise funds without giving away equity, the only option was to go public. To do this, the companies had to hold an Initial Public Offering (IPO). An IPO involves a company selling its private shares to the general public. The shares are usually very cheaply priced, and anyone can buy them. If the company grows, the value of its shares also grows, leading to profits for its investors.

With the rise of cryptocurrencies and blockchain technology, people started wondering if the same IPO model could be replicated on a blockchain based environment. This led to the rise of ICO's, effectively revolutionizing the way companies raise funding and completely changing the tides for startups.

Today, tech startups are raising capital for their projects through the blockchain. People with great ideas are building experienced and competent teams and marketing their idea to the world through the internet. Apart from being a new way to raise capital, this new model has made it possible for anyone to invest in companies they believe in. It does not matter where you are from or how much money you have. If there is a startup that you believe in, you can invest as much as millions of dollars or as little as $50. There are no barriers to investing in ICO's. Anyone can participate in ICO's and make themselves some money.

What Are ICO's?

Initial Coin Offerings are basically a mechanism that companies use for crowd funding. However, instead of selling shares as is the case with IPO's, these companies create and sell digital tokens or coins in exchange for development funds. In addition, ICO's accept cryptocurrencies instead of traditional fiat currency. By owning these coins or tokens, the investors are promised a share of future profits made by the company. One thing that has made ICO's such an attractive investment option is that once the ICO is closed, the tokens are listed for trading on cryptocurrency exchanges. In many cases, the value of these tokens skyrockets once they are listed on the exchanges, leading to investors becoming overnight millionaires.

What Is A Blockchain?

I have mentioned the term blockchain severely, so you might be wondering what it is. The blockchain is a public ledger that keeps a permanent and immutable record of all transactions within a cryptocurrency network. In simpler terms, it is basically a permanent digital spreadsheet that is distributed across several computers. Any changes made to the spreadsheet are validated by all the computers. Each computer then updates its copy of spreadsheet to match these changes. There is no master copy of the blockchain.

What Is A Cryptocurrency?

A cryptocurrency is a virtual or digital currency that depends on the rules of mathematics and cryptography for security. Unlike traditional fiat currencies, cryptocurrencies are not issued or controlled by any central authority, such as a central bank. This means that cryptocurrencies cannot by manipulated by such authorities, including governments. Cryptocurrencies also allow people to make anonymous transactions.

Differences Between ICO's And IPO's

I have mentioned that ICO's are essentially IPO's that are carried out on a blockchain environment. So, what are some of the differences between an ICO and an IPO?

Regulatory Oversight

Before a company can issue an IPO, it must register with a regulatory authority. As part of the registration requirements, the company must create a legal document known as a prospectus. This document establishes certain transparency standards and includes important information about the company and the IPO. This allows people to make informed decisions before investing in the IPO.

Unlike IPO's, there are no legal requirements to regulate ICO's. Instead of a prospectus, companies issuing an ICO create a document known as a whitepaper to provide potential investors with information about the company and the ICO. However, there is no standard for creating whitepapers, therefore the company might include or omit some key pieces of information as they deem necessary.

Credibility And Track Record

Before a company can issue its shares through an IPO, it needs to have a good track record and to meet a certain threshold of minimum earnings. These requirements have to be verified by professional accounting firms. Investment banks also must be involved as underwriters for the deal. All these processes ensure that only credible companies are allowed to offer their shares for sale to the public.

Since most ICO's are simply ideas and companies in the product development phase, they do not have any track record. The only thing backing up the project is the whitepaper. This makes it extremely difficult to assess the fundamentals of the companies. Rather than assessing a company through what it has achieved in the past, ICO's require you to assess a company based on what it promises to do in future. This makes it extremely risky to invest in ICO's. While the experience and competency of the ICO team might be a pointer as to the ICO's credibility, you have no way of determining whether the project will actually be successful.

Utility

When an investor buys the stocks of a company through an IPO, these stocks are the investor's ownership claim to the future earnings of the company. By holding the company's stock, the investor is entitled to receive dividends. The investor also has the right to vote in shareholder's meetings.

On the other hand, ownership of ICO coins does not give an investor any ownership claims into the company. However, there are other ways that the investor may gain future benefits from the ownership of the coins. This depends on the structure of the project. Generally, the value of a coin is directly proportional to the perceived utility of the coin. The more widespread adoption the coin gains, the higher its value is going to rise.

Duration Of Offerings

Owing to the complex legal and compliance processes that they are subjected to, IPO's can be quite lengthy processes. The entire process from acquiring approval from regulatory authorities to the issuance of the IPO normally takes about 4-6 months.

ICO's have a much shorter process. The length of an ICO depends on the nature of the project as well as the timelines put in place by the ICO team. For an ICO to take place, all that has to be done is the creation of a whitepaper and the finalization of the smart contract for the token sale. The length of the token sale depends on the length of time it will take for the ICO to reach its hard cap. Some ICO's might have a fixed sale duration of about a month. However, it is good to keep in mind that well-hyped ICO's might get sold out in a matter of minutes or a few hours.

For instance, the BAT ICO raised $36 million in half a minute.

Access To Offerings

In most cases, IPO's are restricted to institutional investors such as mutual funds, investment banks and endowments. In some cases, a small percentage of the IPO is allocated to retail investors. Therefore, investing in an IPO is extremely hard for those who are not part of that exclusive club. Retail traders can only buy the stocks once they are listed on an exchange.

When it comes to ICO's, anyone can participate. All you need to have is the base currency for the ICO, which is usually either Bitcoin or Ether. This levels the playing field and makes it possible for the masses to participate in and make profits from investments that were typically reserved for the big boys. This is in line with cryptocurrency's concept of breaking down centralization and taking power from the elite club and returning it back to the people.

Characteristics Of An ICO

While each ICO is unique, there are some characteristics that are shared by a majority of ICO's. You will even find some of these characteristics on IPO's. The characteristics of ICO's include:

- The projects or companies issuing ICO's are based on cryptocurrencies or decentralization. Therefore, to invest in ICO's, you need to be familiar with cryptocurrencies and to understand how they work.
- The investor documents that accompany an ICO are the whitepaper, a web page and posts on internet forums. In most cases, the whitepaper is not peer reviewed. There are no rules or standards compelling the ICO to present accurate documents. Because of this, it is not uncommon to find ICO teams that create unsubstantiated hype, fail to identify risks or exaggerate benefits. This is unlike traditional forms of fundraising where strict rules and regulations must be followed to protect the investors.
- Identification is not a requirement. Owing to the anonymous nature of cryptocurrencies, investors contributing to the ICO do not have to identify themselves. No checks are conducted to determine the source of funds or if global financial rules are being followed. Similarly, it is not mandatory for the ICO team to identify itself. However, you should be very wary about investing in ICO's that have anonymous teams.
- While there is transparency in the amount of money raised, ICO's are not safe from gaming. Since ICO's are funded on public blockchains, anyone can access the blockchain to confirm the amount of funds being sent to the ICO address. However, despite this transparency on the amounts being invested in the ICO, there is no way of

identifying the people investing in the fund. This means that some ICO's might self-invest, with the aim of creating an illusion of popularity and momentum, with the aim of generating hype and FOMO (Fear Of Missing Out).

- Most ICO's are tiered, which means that the token sale is done at different tiers. In most cases, ICO's have an early investor advantage, where the earliest investors buy tokens at lower prices. This is usually done by creating time-bound or amount-bound offers for early investors. This characteristic is similar to traditional forms of fundraising where better deals are given to early investors.
- Coin retention and price discovery: In most cases, the project will retain a percentage of the tokens. This is important because it gives the project a valuation. The value of the project is equivalent to the number of retained tokens multiplied by the price per token. In most cases, the project will also declare how the retained tokens will be used.
- Soft and hard caps: Most ICO's usually have minimum and maximum targets for the funds being raised. The soft cap is the minimum target while the hard cap is the maximum cap. If the fundraising fails to meet the minimum target, the amount raised is refunded and the project stops. If the maximum target is met, the ICO closes and any late investments are refunded. Since ICO's are run by smart contracts, all this happens automatically, without the actual involvement of the project team.

How ICO's Work

There is a standard process that all ICO's follow when launching their tokens sales. The process is as follows:

1. The project team comes together and comes up with a blockchain project that is economically viable. The team then announces their intention to create the project. By making the announcement, the team starts generating hype and interest around the project.
2. A whitepaper is developed. The whitepaper gives a description of the technical specifications of the project, the business model and the development schedule that will be followed. The aim of the whitepaper is to entice potential investors. However, instead of being flashy like a brochure, the whitepaper is more formal and is written in an academic manner. Whitepapers are usually more than 2500 words long.
3. The whitepaper is distributed to prominent members of the blockchain community with the aim of getting their backing. This is important because the backing by respected members gives the project credibility.
4. The ICO team develops the coins that are going to be issued to investors in exchange for Bitcoin or Ether. In this stage, the team will have to cover fundamental issues like the maximum number of coins that will be created and the price per coin. The prices are usually quite low. Setting a maximum

number of coins is important because it increases their demand.
5. The team then decides on when the ICO will be held and for how long it will run. They also need to decide on the amount of funds they are targeting, both the soft and the hard cap.
6. The team then embarks on an intense marketing campaign to create more hype for the ICO. This is usually done online through forums, social media, paid ads, YouTube, bloggers and so on.
7. When the ICO date arrives, the token sale launches and the ICO starts accepting contributions. The coins are distributed to investors depending on their contributions.
8. Once the ICO's targets are reached, the ICO closes. The coins are then availed on cryptocurrency exchanges for trading.

Types Of ICO's

ICO's are classified depending on the pricing methods they employ.

Price Increase As More Investors Contribute

These types of ICO's are divided into multiple stages. A specific fixed price is allocated to each stage, with the first stage having the lowest price. As time elapses and as more investors contribute to the project, the ICO moves on to the next stage and the price increases with it. This method rewards early investors who take the most risk.

Price Decrease Over Time

These types of ICO's are also referred to as Dutch auctions. The ICO team sets a high price when the token sale launches. The price of the tokens keeps decreasing as time elapses until all the coins are sold or until a predetermined reserve price is reached. The aim of Dutch auctions is to eliminate the FOMO that usually accompanies contributing to ICO's. An example of a Dutch auction ICO was Gnosis.

Fixed Price

In this type of ICO, there is a fixed exchange rate for the tokens. This type of ICO does not favor early investors or large investors. Once the token sale closes, the coins are then frozen for a set period of time. No one can trade or transfer the coins during this period. Once this cool off period expired, the coins are then listed on exchanges for trading.

Random Price Per Token

In this type of ICO, there is no set price for the tokens. Instead, the project simply accepts contributions from investors. Once the contributions meet the set targets, a token sale is performed and the tokens are distributed to investors according to their contributions.

Before investing in an ICO, you should take the time to understand its terms and conditions. Find out the number of coins that will be issued and the pricing mechanism that the ICO will employ.

Chapter Summary

In this chapter, you have learned:

- That ICO's are a new way for companies to raise funds through cryptocurrency crowdfunding.
- That ICO's came up as a result of applying the principles of ICO's to the blockchain environment.
- That the blockchain is a decentralized public ledger on which cryptocurrencies and ICO's run.
- That cryptocurrencies are virtual currencies that are secured by the rules of cryptography.
- The differences between ICO's and IPO's
- The characteristics of an ICO
- How ICO's work

- The different types of ICO's

In the next chapter, you will learn the advantages and disadvantages of investing in ICO's.

Chapter Two: Advantages And Disadvantages Of Investing In ICO's

In this chapter, you are going to learn the advantages and disadvantages of investing in ICO's. Owing to the soaring of the price of Bitcoin and other cryptocurrencies in the past year and the creation of overnight millionaires from ICO investing, ICO's and cryptocurrencies have been termed as the next big thing. Many people are rushing to put their money into ICO's in an effort to get a share of the pie. While the potential gains of investing in ICO's are enormous, the risks are huge as well. Let us look at some of the advantages and disadvantages of investing in ICO's.

Advantages Of Investing In ICO's

ICO's have a massive potential for returns. The prices of most coins skyrocket immediately after the coins are listed for trading on cryptocurrency exchanges. Those who take a long-term approach to their investments have an even bigger return potential. For instance, if one had invested $1000 in Bitcoin in 2013 when the price of 1 Bitcoin was hovering around $100, their investment today would be worth $100,000. If you had invested in the Spectrecoin ICO in January 2017, your investment would have grown by 13,000%.

ICO's also have shorter time horizons, which means that investors can realize profits and cash out their investments in a relatively short time span. Since Google's IPO in 2004, its share price has grown by 1200% as of February 2018. That is a time frame of 14 years. Compare this to SpectreCoin, which grew by 13,000% within one year. This makes ICO's more attractive than IPO's.

Another advantage of ICO's is that there is a clear direction for execution. Normally, most startups need to pivot several times before they become successful. Therefore, when you invest in a traditional startup, there is a very high likelihood that the company that goes public will be very different from what you initially invested in. With cryptocurrency ICO's, you know exactly what technology you are investing in and what it is supposed to do. There is a clear direction of what the product aims to achieve. Therefore, this makes it easier to make an accurate evaluation of the company you are investing in.

ICO's do not have the restrictions that accompany traditional investments, such as being accredited or having a huge pool of money. This means that anyone, from anywhere, can invest in an ICO provided they are able to transfer their funds on time. This also makes fundraisings completely decentralized, which is a core concept of cryptocurrencies.

By investing in ICO's, you are investing in new or upcoming technology. There is a chance that the ICO you invest in might revolutionize the industry, which makes you a part of something big and potentially translates into huge profits for you. If you carefully analyze and evaluate the ICO's you get into, you might just find yourself on the right startup that will change the world.

With ICO's, apart from simply holding your coins or tokens, you can actually use them to access or pay for the products and services offered by the underlying company. If that particular cryptocurrency becomes popular and gains mass adoption, you might also be able to use it to pay for third-party purchases, similar to how Bitcoin and Litecoin are used to pay for goods and services online.

Most ICO's price their coins at very cheap prices, which makes it possible even for small investors to contribute to the ICO and profit from it once the tokens are listed on cryptocurrency exchanges for trading. Compare this with IPO's, where only people with huge amounts of money can invest.

ICO's are largely unregulated, which makes it easier for investors to get into ICO's and for startups to raise capital. However, with all the buzz they have created in recent times, ICO's have started attracting the attention of regulatory authorities. Already, countries like South Korea and China have already banned ICO's. More countries might choose to go the same route, while others might come up with some way of regulating ICO's. The best thing to do before investing in ICO's is to ensure that you have a clear understanding of the legal position on ICO's in your country. We will look at this in greater detail in Chapter Eleven.

Most ICO's have a cap on the maximum number of coins that will be issued. This creates a limited supply, allowing the cryptocurrency to take advantage of the demand and supply principle. Doing so creates demand for the coins, resulting to an increase in value. This increases the chances of initial investors gaining exponential profits from their investments.

While it is important to have a balanced investment portfolio, it is also good to include some riskier investments – such as venture capital – if you want to see great returns. In today's world, ICO's provide investors with some of the benefits that are lacking in venture capital. Once you take the time to understand ICO's and how they work, you have the possibility of generating massive returns with ICO's.

Disadvantages Of Investing In ICO's

Unlike other investments like real estate and the stock market, ICO markets are very volatile and unpredictable.

Events like the banning of ICO's by China and South Korea can lead to the plummeting of ICO values. There is also the risk of people losing their investments to hackers. While such incidents are exceptions rather than the norm, ICO's are more likely to experience wild fluctuations than traditional investments.

In most cases, investing in an ICO simply means that you are investing in an idea you believe in. Therefore, the real value of your investment relies on the ability of the project team to complete the project successfully. Unless the team can build a strong product that attracts a significant network of users, the tokens will not have any real value, which translates to losses for investors. Most ICO's fail because they are unable to attract network engagement.

There is always the risk of potential mismanagement. Every project issuing an ICO is a startup, with a team of founders running it. In order for the project to successfully move from the ICO stage to mass-adoption, there is need for proper management by the ICO team. This is why, prior to investing in an ICO, it is very important to evaluate the ICO team to determine whether they have the necessary skills and experience to drive the project to success.

When investing in an ICO, there is no guarantee that the project will be completed according to the schedule, or that mainstream users will embrace the technology being offered by the cryptocurrency. Sometimes, the technology being introduced might be years ahead of its time. This means that there is the risk that it might take years before there is an actual real-life demand for the project, which in turn means that it might take years before you see any returns on your investment.

While the lack of regulations makes it easier for people to invest in ICO's, it also means that there is no protection for investors. If something goes wrong, investors will not be reimbursed. Investors cannot take any legal action either. This makes ICO's a lot riskier than traditional investment options. However, the use of smart contracts to lock up ICO funds is making this less of an issue.

The lack of regulation also means that there is no standard that compels ICO's to go through professional vetting. With traditional investments, companies must go through vetting before people can make investments. This vetting provides an analysis of the company's business model and an accurate view of its financial condition, helping investors understand any potential risks about the investment. With ICO's, the only thing investors can assess is the whitepaper and the information provided on the website.

In addition, since you can only assess ICO's based on what they promise to achieve in future, they do not have a proven business model. This makes it quite challenging to make a sound assessment of the project. They are also not bound by geographical boundaries, therefore there is not much investors can do if the ICO team disappears with their money.

Chapter Summary

In this chapter, you have learned:
- ICO's have the potential for massive returns.
- ICO's have shorter time horizons.
- ICO's have a clear direction for execution.
- ICO's are not bound by the restrictions that bind traditional investments.
- By investing in ICO's, you are investing in new or upcoming technology.
- You can also use crypto coins to pay for products and services.
- Getting into ICO's is much easier than traditional investments because they are unregulated.
- Cryptocurrencies have a limited supply, which makes them more valuable.
- ICO markets are volatile and unpredictable.
- By investing in an ICO, you are only investing in an idea. There is no guarantee that the project will be successful.
- There is always the risk of mismanagement.
- The lack of regulation means more risks for investors
- ICO's do not have any proven business model.

In the next chapter, you are going to learn the fundamental factors that affect the value of a cryptocurrency.

Chapter Three: The Fundamental Factors That Affect The Value of A Cryptocurrency

In this chapter, you are going to learn about the factors that affect the value of cryptocurrencies.

When investing in traditional investments like real estate and the stock market, fundamental analysis involves checking the financial statements of the company to assess its financial health and viability. If the statements look good, you can make the decision to invest in the company with the confidence that it has good fundamentals. However, when it comes to ICO's and the cryptocurrencies on which they are based, performing the fundamental analysis is not as straightforward. There are no financial statements to analyze. Analyzing the fundamentals of ICO's and cryptocurrencies is different from analyzing traditional investments because:

- Cryptocurrencies are not corporations. Instead, they are digital assets that represent value within a network. The viability of a cryptocurrency is more dependent on its community (users, miners and developers) rather than on its ability to generate revenue.
- The cryptocurrency space is still in its early stages, and most existing cryptocurrencies are still in their early development stages. This means that very few cryptocurrencies have demonstrated any real-life use case, therefore there is not much of a track record when it comes to evaluating cryptocurrencies.

This means that a different methodology needs to be used to perform the fundamental analysis on cryptocurrencies. Since cryptocurrencies and their underlying technology are a complex phenomenon, it is important to research the viability and potential of the coins before investing. This helps you make more informed decisions with the confidence that you are investing in something worthwhile. To do this, you need to understand the factors that affect the value of a cryptocurrency, which I am going to discuss below.

Factors That Affect The Value Of A Cryptocurrency

Utility

For a coin to be valuable, it needs to have a strong real-world use case or function. If you cannot use the coin, then it has little value. Without a real-life use case, the coin is simply speculative, without being backed by any fundamental value. The better the use case, the more valuable the coin is. Some utilities for crypto coins include being used as a medium of exchange within their respective networks, acting as a claim to dividend payments or giving voting rights to whoever holds the coins.

To illustrate how this works, let's us look at how utility affects the value of some common cryptocurrencies. A good example is Ether, the tokens based on the Ethereum blockchain. For anyone to develop any applications or execute smart contracts on the Ethereum blockchain, you need to have Ether, which acts as the 'fuel' in the Ethereum network. This provides utility for Ether. The more people develop apps and execute smart contracts on the Ethereum network, the more the demand for Ether, which will consequently lead to an increase in the price of Ether. Similarly, Bitcoin is used as a means of payment, which gives it high utility, hence its extremely high price in comparison to other cryptocurrencies.

You should only invest in an ICO if the associated cryptocurrency has a real-life use case.

Scarcity

The value of something depends largely on the laws of supply and demand. Precious metals are some of the most valuable commodities on earth. Their value stems from the fact that they have utility, which increases their demand, and that they are limited in supply. The same rules of supply and demand also apply when it comes to cryptocurrencies. To increase the value of their tokens, most cryptocurrency projects limit the amount of coins or tokens that will be released over the lifetime of the network. This raises the value of the coins as their demand increases. For instance, Bitcoin has a maximum limit of 21 million coins. This means that that if only 1 billion of the 7 billion people in the world were to adopt Bitcoin, its value would be extremely high since they would all have to share only 21 million Bitcoins.

Bitcoin and most other cryptocurrencies also have a mechanism in place that regulates the release of new Bitcoin into the network. This ensures that there is always a limited supply of Bitcoin, thus pushing up its value. Some coins even have a mechanism that 'burns' or destroys a portion of the coins in supply in order to increase their value. When investing in an ICO, check whether there is a maximum supply of the associated coins or tokens.

Perceived Value

A cryptocurrency can only be as valuable as the market perceives it to be. Public perception of a cryptocurrency depends on a number of things. Projects that are backed by reputable people are perceived to be more valuable. Similarly, projects that make partnerships and collaborations with credible companies are perceived to be more valuable. For instance, the perceived value of Bitcoin is high because it was the first cryptocurrency to bring about innovations that threatened to disrupt the traditional banking sector, which is a headache for most people.

Some factors might also lower the perceived value of a cryptocurrency. If a project gets hacked, its perceived value will tank, bringing its actual value down with it. The best way to gauge the perceived value of an ICO is to look at the amount of hype it has generated.

The above are the fundamental factors that affect the value of a cryptocurrency. You should always keep these in mind before you decide to invest in an ICO. However, apart from these, there are some other minor factors that affect the value of a cryptocurrency. These include:

Media

The kind of media attention attracted by the cryptocurrency. If a cryptocurrency is featured in positive light in reputable websites and news channels, then it is likely to be more valuable. On the other hand, negative media attention can lower the value of a cryptocurrency. Sometimes, the media can even be used to manipulate the price of cryptocurrency.

The Price of Bitcoin

Being the market leader in the crypto space, Bitcoin has a huge influence on the performance of the crypto market as a whole. A drop in the price of Bitcoin is usually followed by a drop in the price of most other cryptocurrencies. Investing in an ICO when the price of Bitcoin is falling might mean that the price of the ICO tokens will not surge immediately after the ICO, forcing you to wait much longer before realizing profits. On the other hand, investing in an ICO when the price of Bitcoin is rising can lead to much quicker profits since the market is likely to be bullish.

Innovation

Finally, the innovation brought about by a cryptocurrency also has a bearing on its value. If a coin brings along an innovative solution, then it's likely that its value will be high. However, if a coin is simply a Bitcoin clone that brings nothing new, it's unlikely to have any value. When investing in an ICO, take the time to find out whether the project has any innovations, or whether it is simply another cryptocurrency that is being developed for the sake of cryptocurrency.

Chapter Summary

In this chapter, you learned:
- Valuing cryptocurrencies is different from valuing corporations.
- Cryptocurrencies can only have value if they have a real-life use case.
- ICO's with a maximum token limit will be more valuable.
- The value of a cryptocurrency will also be affected by public perception.
- Media attention can positively or negatively affect the value of a cryptocurrency.
- The price of Bitcoin influences the value of cryptocurrencies and ICO's.
- Innovative ICO's tend to be more valuable.

In the next chapter, you will learn how to choose the right ICO to invest in.

Chapter Four: How To Choose The Right ICO To Invest In

In this chapter, you are going to learn about the considerations you should keep in mind when choosing the right ICO to invest in.

In the last year, the popularity of ICO's has grown tremendously. Nowadays, several ICO's are launched each day, translating to hundreds of ICO's each month. Unfortunately, many of them will not make you any money. You have to practically rummage through the bunch to find the right ones to invest in. So, how do you identify a gem when you come across one?

There are several factors and variables that you should keep in mind when searching for an ICO to invest in. I am going to give you some basic guidelines that you can use to identify great ICO's. Before I get to the guidelines, I will start by saying that I always advocate for making investments for the long term. As much as possible, you should go for projects that have long term value. Avoid short term pump and dump cryptocurrencies, which sadly make up about 95% of the crypto market. With that out of the way, let's look at the factors you need to consider when choosing the best ICO.

Opt For Platforms And Protocols Over dApps

Currently, there are over 1000 cryptocurrencies in existence, with many of them vying for dominance as the best of them all. As the first Cryptocurrency to be developed, Bitcoin is still the most popular Cryptocurrency and the biggest in terms of market capitalization. However, Bitcoin has become outdated. As more people join the Bitcoin network, it has become slow and expensive to use. It does not allow smart contracts to be executed on the network. At the moment, there is a raging debate between Bitcoin core developers and the large mining pools who are trying to make as much money as possible from Bitcoin.

Despite all these challenges, there is something valuable that emerged from Bitcoin – the blockchain, the foundation on which Bitcoin is built. According to most industry experts and leaders in the tech industry, through decentralization, the blockchain will optimize and revolutionize many systems that are currently inefficient. These include systems in fields like supply chain, government, the banking sector, asset management, insurance and many more.

In a few years to come, the real winner might not be Bitcoin, Ethereum, Litecoin or some other coin. Instead, the real winner might turn out to be blockchain technology, because it has the potential to disrupt most of the technology in existence today. Today, people are trying to identify the blockchains that will come out on top and gain widespread adaptation.

Another reason why you should focus on platforms and protocols is that they tend to have the best returns. If a dApp (decentralized application) built on Ethereum solves a real-world problem and gains widespread adoption, it will lead to an increase in the fundamental value of Ethereum. Since there are several dApps being built on each platform, it makes more sense to bet on the entire platform than on one single dApp. To get a good idea of how this works, let's consider a platform like Microsoft Windows. The more applications that are developed on Microsoft Windows, the more valuable it becomes.

Another good way to think of a cryptocurrency platform is to compare it to railroad infrastructure. If you were alive in the 19th century, would you prefer to invest in an individual train or in the railroad infrastructure and get paid rent for every train that used it? How about if you could invest in the HTTP protocol and earn when anyone used the internet? Similarly, it makes a lot more sense to invest in the underlying platform and gain profits as more people use the platform.

According to industry experts, the blockchain will bring the next step in the evolution of the internet. Dubbed Web 3.0, it will provide a safer and more secure foundation on which the new decentralized internet will be built. While we are nowhere near the realization of Web 3.0, that is the future. However, if you believe that Web 3.0 will be based upon blockchain technology, then it is a good move to invest in the infrastructure.

While dApps might have some speculative value, once the frenzy has cooled down, their value will ultimately be pegged on the value of the platform on which they are based. Additionally, platforms are more likely to retain their value in the event that the market turns bearish. The same cannot be said of the dApps.

All in all, you are likely to make bigger profits on platforms and protocols. It's also safer to bet on platforms than dApps. Therefore, when searching for an ICO to invest in, you should lean towards infrastructure projects instead of dApps. If you look at some of the biggest cryptocurrencies by market capitalization, you will notice that a huge fraction of the top 20 list consists of infrastructure projects rather than dApps. This trend is unlikely to stop anytime soon.

Anticipate Market Trends

The most successful people in any sector are those that are able to anticipate and bet on market trends. This rings true whether you are looking at the stock market, forex, commodities, or the Cryptocurrency market. In the Cryptocurrency market, this involves anticipating the direction that the industry is likely to take and investing in cryptocurrencies that are trying to make it easier for the market to follow that direction. This sounds like an easy and very obvious thing to do. However, to be able to do this you need to be knowledgeable about various trends in the Cryptocurrency market and the general state of blockchain technology. This means that you have to closely follow cryptocurrency news and upcoming projects.

For instance, a good way of doing this is anticipating problems that the industry is likely to face and finding cryptocurrencies that are trying to solve these problems. There are some fundamental problems that have become synonymous with blockchain technology today. These problems must be solved before the blockchain can be used to provide solutions for real world problems instead of remaining as a speculative investment. Some of the problems include:

- Scalability (supporting increasing user-base without decrease in transaction speeds)

- Stability (reducing the high volatility. This would allow cryptocurrencies to be used as effective alternatives to fiat currency)
- Interoperability (supporting transactions between different blockchains)

The above three problems are the major bottlenecks to the wide adoption of cryptocurrencies. They have to be solved if cryptocurrencies are to have a future in the real world. Therefore, you are unlikely to go wrong with ICO's that are trying to provide solutions to these problems. Other trends that are likely to get big include:

- Currencies (improved versions of Bitcoin that can be used for daily transactions)
- Alternatives of blockchain technology (such as IOTA)
- Decentralized exchanges
- Money remittance (projects that solve inefficiencies in international money transfers)
- Projects that are trying to optimize the supply chain
- Crypto lending

There is huge potential that projects dealing with any of the above issues will get big. However, these are not the only areas that hold lots of promise. There are many more, and many more potential areas will keep emerging. The best thing you can do is to keep yourself abreast of all industry news and occurrences.

You might come across some people claiming that decentralized apps (dApps) are disruptive and hold a lot of promise. However, I recommend that you avoid investing in dApps. This is because, in most cases, these dApps tend to be money grabs that do not attempt to solve any real-world problem. They solve problems that do not need solving. Most of them can also function without the need for their respective tokens.

At the moment, most cryptocurrencies are extremely overvalued. However, you can expect that there will be a correction in the market. Once this happens, valuation of cryptocurrencies will be based on what each project has achieved, rather than what they promise. There is a high likelihood that this will lead to a collapse in the value of dApps.

The Whitepaper

This is one of the most important things you should look at when evaluating an ICO. The whitepaper is the document that gives a description of what the project wants to accomplish and how they plan on going about it. It contains information about the vision of the project, how their proposed product will work, the developers they have on board and so on. Despite its importance, you would be surprised at the number of investors – especially newbies – who completely ignore the whitepaper. This is a huge mistake.

A high quality ICO should have a clear whitepaper that explains every aspect of the project in a simple, precise and easy-to-understand manner. It should give the exact details on how the team will achieve the project objectives. The more detailed a whitepaper is, the better.

You should be very wary of whitepapers that use extremely technical jargon and 'buzzwords' to explain how their proposed system works and how they plan to implement it. If the ICO team is promising to create a complex system, you want to be sure that they actually know how to go about it.

Who Is Behind The ICO?

Before you put your money into an ICO, you need to do as much research as possible into the team behind the ICO. This is because the team behind the ICO has a very huge impact on the success of a coin. If a team is composed of reputable people who are well known in the tech and cryptocurrency sector, their project is more likely to attract a lot of hype. This is important because it has a significant effect on the value of the coin the first time it hits the exchanges. People who have proved themselves in the crypto industry are also more likely to build something successful. If you were betting at a horse race, would you bet on a renowned jockey who has achieved lots of success previously or would you bet on a virtually unknown jockey? The same way you cannot bet on an unknown jockey, you should not bet your money on an ICO with an unknown team.

I am going to discuss the process of evaluating the ICO team in greater detail in Chapter Six. However, some of the things you should look for include:

- Team members who are not new to the cryptocurrency scene, and who have the experience necessary to deliver what the project is promising.
- Team members who have the right connections (both financial and technical) to see the project to fruition.
- Team members who have either worked for well-known tech companies or who have launched and successfully run their own companies.

If the team has no experience, if you cannot find any successful projects that they run or if you cannot find any history about them, you should be very wary about the ICO. In the unregulated world of ICO's, scammers abound. You do not want to become one of their victims.

As part of your research, you should look at the team members LinkedIn profiles to verify their past work experience. You should also look at the ICO's advisors and verify that through their LinkedIn profiles that they are truly part of the advising team. It is not unusual for scammers to falsely affiliate their ICO's to known personalities without their knowledge. Your research should verify that the ICO team are who they claim to be and that they have the skills and connections to drive the project to success. If you notice any of the team members lying about their experience or if they have falsely listed their advisors, keep away from the ICO. Same case for ICO's without a list of the team members.

Look At The Market Cap

The market cap plays a big role in the amount of returns you are likely to gain from your investments. You should opt for cryptocurrencies that have a low market cap. This is because coins with lower market caps have more room to grow. Going for coins with a low market cap is considered more profitable than going for high cap coins since, for you to make multiple times your initial investments, the market cap of the coin also needs to experience similar increases.

However, this is not to say that you cannot make money on coins that have a high market cap. The cryptocurrency market is wild, and it's not uncommon to see coins rise from a market cap of 10 billion and then jump to 100 billion in a matter of days. However, you should look at the market cap of an ICO before investing. The lower it is, the more likely you are to make big returns. If you think about it, it is easier for an ICO with a market cap of 5 million to experience a 20x gain and rise to 100 million, than it is for one with 100 million to gain 10x and rise to 1 billion.

So, what determines a good market cap?

While there is no hard rule on what makes a good market cap, you can determine a good market cap by looking at the amount of money that is in the market. For instance, if you go back two years ago when the entire crypto market was valued at only a few billion, a market cap of 5 million was extremely high. Fast forward to today when the value of the crypto market is nearing the trillion-dollar mark and 5 million is seen as peanuts.

This shows that to determine a reasonable market cap, you need to look at the total market cap of crypto as well as the current state of the market. The higher the valuation of the crypto market, the more likely it is that ICO's will have a higher market cap from the start. Similarly, the market cap of ICO's is likely to be higher when the market has been experiencing an extended bullish run.

As of January 2018, ICO's with smaller market caps ranged somewhere between $40 and $60 million. ICO's with a market cap of between $60 and $90 million were considered the average, while any ICO exceeding the $90 million mark was definitely in the big leagues.

One thing that you should also keep in mind is that some of the best ICO's with the best teams and huge ambitions are likely to be playing in the big leagues. This means that it would not be surprising if some of the ICO's with insanely huge market caps see big multiples. A good example is Cardano (ADA), which was launched on the 29th of September, 2017. After an extended ICO lockup, Cardano launched with a market cap of about $400 million. By

January 2018, Cardano had joined the top 5 list, with a market cap of over $30 billion. That represents a gain of about 75x. It is likely that a few other ICO's will achieve similar results. However, unless you really believe in a project, its team and what they are out to achieve, I recommend that you should invest in ICO's between $40 and $70 million.

If you see an ICO that checks all the right boxes (the factors discussed in this chapter) and that has a market cap of below $40 million, it is an excellent investment option, with the potential to rake in returns anywhere between 5x and 20x. While lower market cap means a higher chance of getting returns, there's also a limit on how low you should go. I do not recommend investing in an ICO that has a market cap of below $5 million. Investing in such an ICO has the potential for insanely profitable returns, but the risk of losing your money is equally high. This is because most of the ICO's in this bracket tend to be scams. For every high quality ICO in this bracket, you are likely to come across about 20 risky ones.

Remember The Fundamentals

Right now, the cryptocurrency mania has become a hot cake, in similar fashion to what happened prior to the dotcom bubble. Out of FOMO (Fear of Missing Out), everyone, regardless of whether they have the experience or not, is trying to get into the crypto market with the hope of minting themselves some quick millions. Most of these people know very little about the crypto market. They do not know how to trade properly. They do not understand what determines the value of a cryptocurrency. Most of them are only armed with the little knowledge they have learned from a couple of online articles. Some invest based on the advice of someone they met at the bar or gym.

The effect of such an influx of inexperienced investors is that they spur the market to higher and higher levels. As they flock into the market, eager to make a quick buck, they push up the demand of the coins, and the price goes up with it. Unfortunately, most of these people do not know much about the coins they are actually investing in. They do not understand any of the fundamentals of the crypto market. The result is that some virtually worthless coins get to astronomical market caps. This is because the coins have no fundamental value. Instead, their prices are driven by the speculative value assigned to them due to the increasing demand.

Some of these coins have no real purpose. Others promise ideas that are not practical, owing to either technological or societal barriers. Yet, others are plain cash grabs. Once the speculative mania comes to an end and the market starts valuing these coins based on their real-world applications, the prices of such coins will collapse, leading to heavy losses for people who had invested in them. To avoid this, you should ensure that you only invest in ICO's that have fundamental value, those that have a good reason for their existence.

Check The Hype Meter

Advertising is a huge factor in the success of any traditional company. Similarly, advertisement is just as important in the crypto world. The more hype that an ICO can generate, the higher the returns its investors will get. With the right amount of hype, it is not uncommon for ICO's to see multiple gains right out of the gate (2x, 5x, 10x and so on). Therefore, before investing in an ICO, check the sort of hype it has generated so far. Some of the things you can look at include:

- Articles about the ICO that have been posted on reputable websites.
- Social buzz (tweets from influencers, huge Reddit discussions, YouTube videos) generated by the ICO.
- The size of the ICO's Slack and Telegram channels.
- The number of people joining the ICO's Telegram channel each day.

Unmet Demand

Another factor you should look at to determine whether an ICO is worth investing in is the unmet demand of the ICO.

By this, I mean that you should check whether there are people who want to put their money into the ICO but are unable to do so for one reason or another. In most cases, unmet demand usually arises from the ICO having a whitelist. A whitelist is a special email list that you must sign up for, prior to the launch of the ICO, in order to be allowed to participate in the ICO.

Why is this important?

If an ICO has generated adequate hype and demand around it but a lot of people cannot participate because of a whitelist, these people will rush to buy as soon as the coins hit the exchanges. This means that the price is likely to skyrocket post ICO, which translates to bigger returns for you.

So, how can you determine if an ICO has a huge unmet demand? Below are some of pointers that you can use to identify ICO's that are likely to shoot skyward immediately they hit the market.

- The ICO requires a whitelist for participation
- The whitelist is hard to obtain
- The whitelist is limited (only a certain number of people can sign up)
- The whitelist filled up quickly and closed
- Strict KYC (Know Your Customer) rules

Apart from the whitelist, you should also look at the performance of the presale. Ideally, you want an ICO with a presale that sold out quickly and one that gave little or no bonuses in the presale. If an ICO gives out huge bonuses during the presale, there's a high likelihood that the investors will dump their coins at ICO price or below ICO price after the ICO, since they will still make a profit. Some of the ICO's that have seen the biggest returns are those that did not hold any public ICO, because the ICO was completely sold out during the presale. This leads to a huge unmet demand and an explosion of prices immediately after the ICO hits the exchanges.

Therefore, if you want to gain huge profits, go for an ICO with lots of unmet demand. The higher the number of willing buyers who are unable to participate in the ICO, the more demand the coin will have post ICO.

Is There Any Working Product Or Prototype?

Another factor you can use to evaluate the potential of an ICO is to identify if it has a prototype. This is because having a prototype means that the project is close to delivering the actual product. However, this does not mean that you should automatically ignore any project that does not have a prototype or a working product. There are several high value cryptocurrencies that do not have any prototype or working product. For instance, IOTA is just an idea, with no actual product. The product is years away from being practical and usable. Cardano, which is valued at $10 billion, does not have any working product. It does not even have a mainnet (a live public network for the cryptocurrency) or a testnet (a beta test network). Actually, a huge percentage of all altcoins do not have any working product or prototype.

This means that you will limit your choices and possibly miss some potential big wins if you decide to focus only on ICO's with a working product. Looking for ICO's with a prototype simply helps you reduce your risk. This consideration is important when the market is bearish, since it helps you reduce the risk of going into ICO's that turn out to be flops. However, if the market is bullish, this consideration becomes less important. If an ICO does not have any prototype, you should look at the project team and try to determine if they are capable of delivering whatever they are promising.

Chapter Summary

In this chapter, you learned:
- You should opt for platforms and protocols over dApps.
- You should anticipate market trends and invest in ICO's that follow that direction.
- You should go through the ICO whitepaper.
- You should research the identity and competency of the ICO team.
- The market cap influences the returns you are likely to make from an ICO.
- You should never ignore the fundamentals.

- The more hype an ICO generates, the more the returns you are likely to see from the ICO.
- Choose ICO's that have high unmet demand.
- Check whether the ICO has a prototype or working product.

In the next chapter, you will learn how to evaluate an ICO's whitepaper.

Chapter Five: How To Evaluate An ICO's White Paper

In this chapter, you are going to learn about the things you should look for when evaluating an ICO's whitepaper.

The decision on whether to invest in an ICO or not depends largely on the ICO's whitepaper. The whitepaper is a document that outlines and explains everything concerning the ICO – what it aims to achieve, what you stand to gain by investing in the ICO, the team behind the ICO, how they plan to achieve the project objectives, and so on.

You can think of the whitepaper as a business plan for the ICO. Entrepreneurs cannot raise capital for their businesses without a business plan. Similarly, an ICO cannot raise funds without a whitepaper. Investors would not be willing to put their money into a project without the proper information about the project and the experience of the team members. For this reason, whitepapers need to impress the reader.

While every ICO has a whitepaper, the problem is that whitepapers are as diverse as the ICO's they represent. Whitepapers do not have any universal structure, standard or best practice. This makes it difficult to tell a good whitepaper from a bad one, especially if you are new to ICO's. How do you tell if an ICO is good by looking at the whitepaper? Below are some of the things you should look for when reading a whitepaper.

The product: The first thing you want to find out is what the team building. Is the software in development, do they have a prototype that you can test or a working product? Is their product still an idea? When can you expect a finished, fully functioning product? Ideally, you should lean towards ICO's that have already started the development of their product. If they have a beta version that you can test, that's even better. You should also consider they type of tokens that will be issued during the ICO. There are two main types of tokens:

- **Usage tokens**: These are tokens that give you the ability to use a certain product or service. While you do not have any special rights, you are guaranteed access to the service. Examples of usage tokens include Bitcoin and Ether.
- **Work tokens**: These are tokens that give you certain rights in a decentralized autonomous organization (DAO), such as voting rights.

Examples of work tokens include Augur and Maker.

Before you participate in the ICO, find out the type of tokens and identify what you will gain by owning these tokens.

Vision: What is the project trying to accomplish? Is there a real-world use case for the product? How do they plan to accomplish the project objectives? Is there a road map? How realistic is the roadmap? Ideally, you should go for ICO's that have a detailed course of action for the next 12 to 18 months. This plan should include a beta launch at the very least.

Value: What is the value of the tokens being issued? Can they be exchanged for goods and services? If it cannot be exchanged for goods and services, how can you be sure that the token is not a scam? How is the product or service being developed different from others that are currently in the market?

Team: Who are the people working on this project? Are they experienced in this field? Do they have a proven track record? Are they working on the project full-time or part-time? Are they volunteering or working on contract? Are they recognized personalities in the tech/crypto world? The team is actually more important than the idea. If an idea is not working, the right team can pivot the objectives of the project and still deliver a successful product. On the other hand, the wrong team is unlikely to achieve success, even when they have a killer idea.

Problem vs. solution: What problem is the project trying to solve? Does the problem actually need solving? How big is the problem – is it a large-scale problem or a niche problem? What solution is the project providing? Is it workable and sustainable? Are there competitors trying to solve the same problem. How is the solution different from those provided by the competitors? Can the solution work outside the blockchain? Is the project simply riding on the blockchain trend when it could provide a better solution without relying on blockchain technology?

Technology: If you are technically savvy, try to determine whether the claims being made by the ICO team are valid. Can the team do what they claim it can do? Is their roadmap achievable within the set time frame? Are there some potential pitfalls that the team has not considered?

Investment yield: How many coins will be issued during the ICO? The more the coins that will be issued, the less the value of each individual coin. This in turn reduces your potential gains. Is the coin really worth investing in?

Terms: Find out the terms of the ICO. What percentage of the coins will be allocated to the project team? Avoid ICO's where the largest share is allocated to the core team. This is one of the red flags that indicate that the ICO might be a scam.

How the funds will be used: Find out how the team plans to use the funds raised during the ICO. If you find anything suspicious in how the team plans to use the funds, there is a high chance that the ICO is trying to fleece investors.

Exchange listing: Find out when the tokens will be listed on an exchange. If the team does not have a detailed plan or if the listing schedule exceeds 60 days after the close of the ICO, be very wary of the ICO.

Underlying ecosystem: How strong is the ecosystem that the token is based on? Examples of ecosystems include Bitcoin, Ethereum, JavaScript, Node.js, Golang, C++, and so on.

Risk of fraud: Watch out for any red flags that the ICO might be a scam. The factors that you should watch out for to avoid getting scammed will be discussed in greater detail in Chapter Ten.

Chapter Summary

In this chapter, you learned:
- You should find out what the team is building.
- You should find out the vision of the team, what they are trying to accomplish.
- You need to determine the value of the tokens being issued.
- You need to check the competency of the team.
- You need to determine whether the ICO is solving a problem that actually needs solving.
- You should verify whether the claims being made by the ICO team are valid.

- You need to determine the potential investment yield of the ICO.
- You should find out the terms of the ICO.
- The team needs to spell out how they plan to use the funds raised in the ICO.
- The team should specify when the tokens will be listed on an exchange.
- You should check the strength of the underlying ecosystem.
- You should watch out for any red flags that the ICO might be a scam.

In the next chapter you will learn how to evaluate the ICO team.

Chapter Six: How To Evaluate The ICO Team

In this chapter, you are going to learn the questions you need to ask yourself when evaluating the ICO team.

In Chapter Four, I mentioned that you should check the ICO team to find that they are who they claim to be and that they are capable of seeing the project through to success. Researching on the ICO team goes beyond searching for their names on Google and checking their LinkedIn profiles. You need to understand what makes a team member valuable to the ICO. Sure, they might have worked for Google or Intel before, and that's good, but does their experience make them qualified for this particular project? When researching an ICO team, below are five questions you need to answer before you put your money into the ICO.

Is The Management Team Capable Of Implementing The Solution?

You can easily determine the strength of a team by looking at the strength of its leaders. A time without a great leader is unlikely to achieve success. Therefore, you need to pay special attention to the management (leaders) of the ICO team and find out if they are capable of steering the project to success. What are their past endeavors? Have they held any leadership roles before?

Find out if the leaders have tried business in the past. Did they succeed? If they did not, why did they fail? While past failure does not predict future failure, you want to watch out for any red flags that might show that the management team is not qualified to lead the project to success. Were they unaccountable? Did they lack the right management skills? However, keep in mind that some failures may be have occurred with valid reasons, such as lack of capital or having the wrong partners. Take the time to dig deeper.

You should also keep in mind that the management is in charge of the rest of the team. They might even choose to replace some members of the team. Therefore, you need to be sure that the project has the right management team. If the management team is great, there is a likelihood that the rest of the team is great too.

How Did Their Past Experience Prepare Them For This Role?

ICO's are usually run in the initial stages of the project when the project team is usually quite small. With a small team, it usually means that each member has to play a much wider role. Therefore, you need to be sure that each member of the team is experienced enough to take care of all the project requirements on their side.

A good way of determining that a team member has enough experience to cover the diverse requirements of a project in its initial project is to look at their career progression. Ideally, you want team members who have had a natural career transition. When looking at the experience of the team members, find out whether they have worked from junior roles and naturally progressed to leadership roles. Such people are likely to have more experience in diverse areas. You should be wary of team members who have only been hired directly into leadership positions.

Another good way of evaluating the experience of the members it to check if they have any practical expertise in the field. Do they have any personal achievements? Have they created anything before? Is this their first experience in this field? Ideally, you want leaders who have successfully run businesses before, marketers who have a great portfolio to show and developers who are active on Github.

What Qualifies Them To Successfully Deliver This Project To Market?

To be able to build a product that successfully meets customer needs, the team members need to have skills geared towards that particular market. Members who have previously worked in the domain have better knowledge of market needs. They understand the problems faced by customers in that domain and they know best how to solve these problems. Therefore, you should go for projects that have such members in their ICO team. If you notice that a project is trying to provide a solution for a particular problem but does not have any members who have adequate experience in that industry, there is a high likelihood that the project is headed for failure.

Is There Anything Missing From The Team?

After you have done your due diligence on the current members of the ICO team, the next step is to identify if there are any missing links. Is there a role that is not covered? How important is this role? If it's important, are there any plans to have it filled? A good way to identify missing links is to look at the jobs/careers page. Have they posted any open positions? What is the description accompanying the post? Are they currently looking for the right person to fill the gap? When was it posted? If you find that a position has been unfilled for more than three months, you should treat that as a red flag. Some of the key roles you should consider in this stage include:

Engineers and developers: Does the team have enough engineers and developers? Ideally, there should be more than one. A team with only one technical member will be slow in development and implementation of changes and upgrades. The project will also be biased to his personal flaws.

Designer: A designer is an important member of the team if they want to build an attractive product that users will love. While a project might choose to hire a freelancer, it is always better when there is a full-time designer.

Marketing expert: For the project to be successful, it needs someone to increase its visibility, increase engagement and attract potential investors.

Community manager: An active community manager helps to build loyalty for the product from both customers and investors.

A market expert: Remember, I mentioned that a project can only succeed if at least one of the members is experienced in the industry for which the team is trying to build a product.

These are not the only roles you should look for, but they are some of the most important. Other roles you can look for include product manager, communication, sales and so on.

What Is The Role Of The ICO's Advisors?

Aside from the list of the team members who are actually involved in the project, ICO's also post a list of the project advisors. Sometimes, the roles of these advisors are not made clear. It's always important to identify the role played by the advisors. Do they supervise the decision made by the project team, or are they merely supporting the project? Sometimes, projects will add a renowned person to their advisors list when the person is not actually playing any active role in the project. For instance, after Ethereum gained popularity, some projects started including Vitalik Buterin – Ethereum's founder – in their advisor's list. Although they did this with his approval, Vitalik was not giving any actual advice on how these projects were run. Instead, his name merely showed that he believes in the project team and what they are doing. While having the support of a big name in the industry is a plus for the ICO, such an advisor does not add any actual value into the project.

Therefore, it's important to identify the actual relationship between the project and each advisor. One way of doing this is to look for articles speaking about the advisor's involvement in the project. You can also look at his social media accounts to see if he is actually following the project and sharing his insights on the progress of the project. If big name advisors are truly involved in the project, this can lead to an increase in the value of the ICO. On the other hand, you should watch out for and avoid ICO's that try to present advisors as part of the core project team.

As I close this chapter, I want to make it clear that it is next to impossible to have a perfect ICO team. Therefore, you should not dismiss an ICO at the first sign of a red flag. These are only some of the things you should watch out for. If anything makes you feel uneasy about the project team, take the time to dig deeper and confirm or disprove your suspicions.

Chapter Summary

In this chapter, you have learned:

- How to verify whether the management team is capable of implementing the solution.
- How to determine whether the team's past experience has prepared them for their role in the ICO.
- You need to check whether there is anything missing from the team.
- You should check the ICO's advisors and their role in the project.

In the next chapter, you are going to learn how to evaluate the ICO's market projections and competitor analysis.

Chapter Seven: Evaluating An ICO's Market Projections And Competitor Analysis

In this chapter, you are going to learn how to evaluate the ICO's market projections and determined whether they provide an accurate description of the market or whether they are an exaggeration.

Now that you have looked at an ICO's whitepaper, researched the project team, looked at the project fundamentals and confirmed that everything is solid, the next thing you need to do is to evaluate the market to ascertain that there is indeed a reasonable market for whatever product or service the project plans to offer. It is not uncommon for a great team to come together to implement a great idea, only for them to fail because of targeting a very small market.

In most cases, the ICO team will have done its own market research, and most times you will find that their research is solid. However, to avoid losing your money, it's important to do your own evaluation to confirm whether their research makes sense. Since ICO's are essentially startups, we are going to look at the same parameters that are used to evaluate the market for other startups outside the crypto space. Below are the parameters you need to be familiar with:

Total Addressable Market (TAM)

The Total Addressable Market refers to the total number of people that could possibly use whatever product or service the project is developing. Let's look at a project like Storj, which is creating a decentralized cloud storage solution. In this case, the TAM for Storj would be all the people in the world that would like to use cloud storage services.

Serviceable Available Market (SAM)

While the TAM gives the total number of people who would be possibly interested in a product or service, it is not a very accurate representation of the actual market. For one reason or the other, the company will not be able to reach all these people. The reasons behind this could be things like geographical, social or technological limitations.

The Serviceable Available Market takes into account such limitations and only considers the market that the company can actually reach. For instance, they might only limit themselves to the portion of the market that speaks English. The criteria used to narrow down to the SAM depends on the company and the product or service being created.

Serviceable Obtainable Market (SOM)

The SAM is a good figure because it helps the project determine the total number of people it can reach. However, it is still impossible to reach all these people. This is because some of them will be using a competitor's product. For instance, if we go back to our Storj example, a huge portion of the market will be using existing services like One Drive, Drop Box, Google Drive and so on. It would be next to impossible for Storj to steal all users from all these companies.

This is where the Serviceable Obtainable Market comes in. This refers to the portion of the market share that the ICO company thinks it can gain. Here, you need to be careful since some companies might exaggerate the numbers. Gaining 5% of the market share is reasonable. Gaining 10-20% is still doable. However, be wary of companies claiming that they expect to gain over 50% of the market share or more. This is not something that can be done easily. It also takes time. When you come across such an ICO, there is a high likelihood that their market research is not accurate. You could even be looking at an ICO that is trying to scam investors.

Compound Annual Growth Rate (CAGR)

This figure is an expression of the average annual growth that the company expects to experience over the next couple of years. This figure can help you determined how you expect your returns to grow over the years. This is another figure that you need to watch keenly. In an attempt to lure investors, some companies will inflate their CAGR. Just like the SOM, a CAGR of 10-20% is reasonable. However, figures of about 50% or more might be an exaggeration. Such growth is not easily achievable.

Go-To-Market Strategy (GTM Strategy)

This refers to the specific action plan that the company intends to follow to achieve a competitive edge and achieve its SOM projections. The GTM strategy provides a blueprint for how the company will get the product into the market and takes into consideration factors like pricing and marketing.

Now that you have a clear understanding of the factors that affect the potential market of an ICO, it's time to go over the market research data provided by the company. Look at the different figures given and check whether they make sense. If possible, try to validate the information on your own.

Analyzing The Competition

Apart from looking at the market size that the ICO is targeting, it's equally important to evaluate the competition that the ICO is going to face. Are there any competitors in the market? Are the competitors blockchain-based or traditional? What benefits does the ICO offer over its competitors? What sets it apart from the rest? Without conducting proper competitor analysis, it is impossible to come up with accurate figures for factors like the SOM and will lead to an ineffective GTM strategy.

If you find that a whitepaper does not include any competitor analysis, this is usually a sign that the company has not done enough market research. If the company claims that it has no competitors, you should treat this as a red flag. This could be an indication that they are trying to solve a problem that does not need solving.

When evaluating the market projections and competitor analysis, do not take anything at face value. Verify for yourself that the information is accurate and that it makes sense.

Chapter Summary

In this chapter, you have learned:

- The parameters that are used to determine evaluate an ICO's market projections.
- How to analyze the competition

In the next chapter, you will learn how to participate in ICO's.

Chapter Eight: How To Participate In ICO's

In this chapter, you are going to learn how to begin to participate in ICO's. Having learned everything you need to know about how to evaluate ICO's and how to pick winners, you are now ready to get into one. Below are the steps involved in participating in an ICO.

Research Upcoming ICO's

Before you can participate in ICO's, you need to know the ICO's that are coming up. This is important since it helps you to plan ahead, to prepare your money and to join the ICO whitelist if there is any. There are several news outlets and resources where you can keep yourself up to date on upcoming ICO's. I am going to share such resources in Chapter Twelve.

Perform Your Due Diligence

Using the steps discussed in the previous chapters, perform your own evaluation of the ICO. Read the whitepaper, research on the ICO team, evaluate the market projections and competitor analysis and ensure that the fundamentals are solid. Apart from doing your own evaluations, you can also go through analysis done by industry experts to ascertain the potential of the ICO.

Open An Exchange Account And Obtain Ether

Once you have performed your due diligence and you are confident that you want to take part in the ICO, the next thing you need to do is to create an account with a cryptocurrency exchange. ICO token sales do not accept payments in traditional fiat currencies since they are designed to work with smart contracts that automatically accept contributions and then send the ICO tokens. Therefore, you need to convert your fiat currency to a cryptocurrency. You can convert your convert your fiat currency into Bitcoin Ether. Most ICO token sales today are run on the Ethereum network, therefore your best bet is to obtain some Ether.

There are several cryptocurrency exchanges where you can convert your dollars into Ether. Some common ones include Coinbase, Kraken and cex.io. You should begin the sign-up process on the exchange platforms at least one week prior to the token sale. This gives you enough time to have your account set up and to purchase the Ether in readiness for the ICO.

Set Up Your Wallet

One of the biggest mistakes that most newbies make when participating in an ICO is to contribute funds from their exchange account. This does not count as your own wallet. Cryptocurrency exchanges do not assign you a single wallet address when you sign up for an account. Instead they assign you a different address every time you want to receive funds. On the other hand, when you contribute funds to an ICO, the ICO tokens are sent to the same wallet that sent the contribution. If you make a contribution from your exchange account, you will not receive your tokens. Instead, you will only make the exchange richer.

What you need to do is to create your own personal wallet where you have control of your private keys. Some good examples of wallets that you should consider using are MyEtherWallet and Parity. Setting up your own personal wallet through either of these services is quite easy.

Register For The Whitelist

With some ICO's, being signed up to the whitelist prior to the launch of the ICO is a requirement for participation in the ICO. Whitelists have become a common trend among ICO's that are popular with a limited number of tokens to offer. If the ICO you want to invest in has a whitelist, you cannot take part without being enrolled in the whitelist.

In most cases, there are some criteria that are used to determine whether someone can enroll in the whitelist. For instance, some whitelists prevent people from some jurisdictions from joining, such as the USA and China. To enroll to the whitelist, you will also be required to provide some personal information. Sometimes, you might also be required to submit a copy of your passport in compliance with KYC (Know Your Customer) laws. In addition, some whitelists will also require you to state the amount of tokens you intend to purchase during the ICO. Generally, most ICO's have a maximum cap on the number of tokens that each investor can purchase.

Things To Keep In Mind Before The Token Sale

Once you have successfully enrolled into the ICO whitelist, you are now ready to get into the ICO. However, before you proceed, you should carefully go through the terms and conditions of the ICO. You should also go through the provided step-by-step guidelines on how to take part in the ICO. Make sure you have also joined the ICO's official Telegram and Slack channels in order to stay up-to-date on any news about the ICO. You should also keep in mind that ICO's are usually opened for a limited time frame. This is either stated by block numbers or by the actual specific time. If the ICO initiator has provided specific block numbers, you can use the Ethereum block explorer to keep track of the block numbers. If they have provided a specific time, check the time zone and synchronize it with yours.

Contribute To The ICO

Now that you are through with all the ICO prerequisites, it is time to actually take part in the ICO by sending your funds to the ICO address.

Before sending your funds to the ICO address, you should note that there are scams floating online where some people will try to fool investors into sending their Ether to the wrong address. Once crypto coins have been sent, there is no way for you to retrieve them, therefore you need to ensure that you are contributing to the correct address. The best way to confirm that you are sending to the correct address is to check the ICO address from the company website. Do not get the ICO address from the Slack channel, since it is possible for a scammer to share the wrong address by pretending that they are a community manager. While there is a possibility that the company site might be hacked, it remains the best place to get the right ICO address.

Once you are sure that you have the correct address, you can now go ahead and send the amount of Ether you want to contribute to the ICO address. Most token sales are built on the ERC-20 standard, therefore you should be able to receive the ICO tokens on the same wallet you used to contribute to the ICO. If there is a compatibility issue for some reason, the company will have posted guidelines on how investors can secure their ICO tokens.

While sending your Ether to the ICO address, you will be required to pay 'gas' for the transaction. You will notice a field on the transaction page asking you to set the gas limit. You might be wondering what this means. Normally, when you engage in any transaction on the Ethereum blockchain, you have to pay some transaction fees. These fees are referred to as 'Gas'. These transaction fees are paid to the miners who validate and confirm transactions on the network. The higher your gas limit, the faster your transaction is likely to be confirmed.

Once you are done sending your contribution to the ICO address, in most cases, you will immediately receive the ICO tokens on your wallet. Some ICO's will require you to wait for a few days before receiving your tokens. Other ICO's might also ask you manually redeem your tokens.

Secure Your Tokens

Once you receive the ICO tokens to your wallet, it is advisable to move them to a more secure wallet. If you intend to hold the tokens for a long time, I would recommend keeping them in a cold wallet. Cold wallets provide the most secure way of holding your cryptocurrencies.

Exchanges To Trade ICO Coins

If you believe in the ICO you invested in, and the tech behind it, the best option is to hold the coins until you hit your targets (2x, 5x, 10x, 50x growth and so on). However, if your intention is to flip the ICO coins, you can start trading the coins immediately after they hit the exchanges. Similarly, if you were unable to take part in the ICO for some reason, you can buy the ICO coins from the exchanges. Some of the most popular exchanges where you can buy or sell ICO tokens include:

Ether Delta: This is a decentralized exchange that allows users to trade in most Ethereum-based tokens. Ether Delta is usually among the first exchanges to list newly issued ICO tokens. However, Ether Delta is a bit complicated. Beginners might find using Ether Delta to be a challenge.

Bittrex: This is a very popular cryptocurrency exchange that is also the biggest by trade volume. Bittrex does not accept traditional currencies. Owing to its popularity and huge trade volume, this is one of the big-league exchanges where every ICO aspires to be listed.

Liqui.io: This is an exchange where you will find most newly issued ICO tokens.

Binance: This is another huge and popular cryptocurrency exchange that is based in Malta. Binance lists newly issued tokens based on the amount of demand they have generated.

Poloniex: This is among one of the biggest exchanges by trade volume. Just like Bittrex, Poloniex does not accept traditional currencies. Being one of the biggest exchanges, most ICO's also aspire to be listed here, though Poloniex has very tough criteria for accepting newly issued coins.

Chapter Summary

In this chapter, you learned:

- You need to research upcoming ICO's.
- Yu should perform due diligence before participating in the ICO.
- You need to open an exchange account and obtain Ether.
- You should use a personal wallet rather than the exchange account when contributing to the ICO.
- You need to enroll to the whitelist if the ICO has one.
- Things to keep in mind before the token sale.
- How to contribute to the ICO.
- You should move your tokens to a safer wallet.

- Popular exchanges where you can trade ICO tokens.

In the next chapter, you will learn the best strategies to make a fortune on ICO's.

Chapter Nine: Best Strategies To Make A Fortune On ICO's

In this chapter, I am going to teach you the strategies that I have personally used to make myself a fortune through ICO's.

Now that you have learned how to choose the right ICO's to invest in, how to evaluate market projections and how to participate in ICO's, in this chapter I am going to give you some general tips that you can use to make yourself a fortune by investing in ICO's. While this list is not comprehensive, it contains a set of great rules that you should follow when investing in ICO's. Let's dive in.

Go Long Instead Of Short

After investing in a coin that has solid fundamentals, a great vision and a team you believe in, I recommend that you hold it for the long term is you want to gain huge returns. Sure, there is money to be made by swing trading or day trading, but if you want the biggest ROI, you should hold your coins. The crypto market is wild. It is ultra-fast and highly volatile. In a week, the crypto market can go through swings that would take the stock market years to experience. You can earn more returns in the crypto market in three months than you would earn in 10 years in the stock market.

As a result of the fast pace of the crypto market, and the quick wins that transform people into millionaires in a matter of days, people have become very impatient. They are not willing to hold their coins for an extended period of time. Instead, they try to increase their investments by flipping them into whatever coin is bullish at the time. However, if you want to make the most out of your investments, you should hold it for the long term.

If you ask most seasoned investors what they regret doing in their early days, most will say that their number one regret is selling early. You might buy a coin at .50c and sell it $3, only for it to continue rising to $10. When you sell early, you lose out on the greater gains that come as the coins continues developing. If you want to see 20x, 50x, 100x or even 1000x returns on your investment, you should hold your coins for several months, and sometimes years.

Cryptocurrencies gain their value as development milestones are achieved and as they make notable partnerships within the industry. This does not happen in a matter of days. If a coin has solid fundamentals and a great team, you can expect that it will continue growing over several months and years. As the phrase goes, time in the market beats timing the market.

Only Invest In Coins You Believe In

One of the biggest mistakes made by newbies is putting their money into an ICO they know little or nothing about. I mentioned above that to gain maximum returns from your investment, you need to hold your coins for months, and sometimes years. To do this, you need to have an unshakeable belief in the coin you invested in. Without such a belief, you will be pressured to sell as the market conditions change or when the market is extremely bearish. However, if you believe in your coin and its fundamental value, you will be confident that the price will go up despite prevailing market conditions.

You Might Find Gems In ICO's That Don't Reach Their Hard Cap

In Chapter Four, I mentioned that the market cap of an ICO is a key factor for determining the amount of returns you can expect from your investment. The lower the market cap, the more likely you are to take home huge profits. ICO's usually have two categories of market cap:

Hard cap: This is the maximum amount of funds that an ICO can raise.

Soft cap: This is the minimum amount of funds required for an ICO to be termed as successful. If an ICO does not meet its soft cap, it gets cancelled and the investors receive back their funds.

In most cases, ICO's that are well hyped will quickly meet their hard cap. However, sometimes some quality ICO's are unable to meet their hard caps. This usually happens during market corrections or when market conditions are bearish. Sometimes, some ICO's will barely meet their soft cap. Such ICO's have lots of potential for growth once market conditions improve. If you are willing to take the risk and put your money into such ICO's, you can easily take home good returns. However, to get good returns with such coins, you must be ready to hold them for several months. You are unlikely to earn any profits if you try to flip such coins for immediate profit.

When looking for ICO's that did not meet their hard cap, you must be very careful. Take the time to evaluate the ICO using the strategies discussed in previous chapters to ensure that it is indeed a quality ICO. If you do not do this, you might end up with a dud. Examples of winners that started as 'failed' ICO's include Dragonchain and AION. You are most likely to come across such ICO's during bear markets.

Always Take Some Profit

The crypto market is wildly volatile. You can easily make millions in a few days. Similarly, you can also lose your whole investment in a few days or hours. To avoid losing your entire investment, you should always take some profit. Apart from selling too early, the second biggest regret for most cryptocurrency investors is losing out on gains because of failing to sell just before a market correction.

This piece of advice might feel contradictory with my first guideline, where I said that you should be prepared to hold your coins for the long term. To help you find a balance between holding and taking some profit, you should come up with an investment strategy where you take a specific percentage of profit once your coin achieves certain profit milestones. For instance, you can decide to sell a certain percentage of your investment every time your coin grows by certain multiples. Decide on your specific strategy and stick to it. Having such a strategy will keep you from selling too early, while at the same time keeping you from losing all your profits due to a market correction.

For instance, you might decide that you will sell 10% of your investment once the coin grows by 10x. This way, you recoup your initial investment and remain with 90% of your coin stash. From there, you might decide to sell 5% or 10% every time the value of the coin increases by 2x. This way, you will continue profiting without selling out your entire stash too early, and you stand to gain significant gains in case the coin shoots to the moon after holding for a long time.

There is no hard rule on what profit-taking formula you should follow. You should come up with your own formula depending on your level of risk tolerance. However, by taking some profit, it becomes easier to hold your coins since you have recouped your initial investment. You will also be periodically locking in your profits, which means that you won't have much regrets in case the market the market takes a dip later on.

Go Big On Promising ICO's, Avoid The Rest

It is always better to place a huge investment on a winner than to place several small investments on average ICO's. Consider this, if you had $10,000 to invest, would you rather put $1000 into ten ICO's that give you a 5x return on average, or would you put the entire amount into one ICO that gives you a 50x return? Putting $1000 into 10 ICO's with 5x average returns would earn you only $50,000. On the other hand, investing the entire sum in one ICO with 50x returns would earn you $500,000. This shows it is better to make big investments on winners.

You need to keep in mind that finding such winners is the real challenge. If it was easy, everyone would be a millionaire. Therefore, you need to do the proper research to ensure that you find ICO's that have a high likelihood of winning. If you find one that looks like a winner, do not be afraid to place a big investment on it.

Take Advantage of Presales To Make Money

There is one little secret that most people trying to invest in ICO's are not aware of. By the time a coin gets to the ICO stage, some people have already made their money. Normally, most ICO's have four stages: the private sale, the presale, the public sale (ICO) and exchange stage. The earlier you get in, the more profits you make. By the time you get in at the ICO stage, you will be up against other investors who got the coins at a lower price. This is because most ICO's allow big investors (whales) to invest in the coins before the public ICO. Additionally, most of these presales are usually accompanied by huge bonuses. This means that those who buy coins during the presale get more coins for the same price than those who buy during the public ICO.

Presales also allow you to buy large allocations of the coins. During the ICO stage, investors are limited to buying only a small allocation of the coin, usually equivalent to just a few ETH. However, during the presale, you can buy a larger amount of coins. This is the perfect way of turning thousands into millions of dollars.

So, how do you get into a presale?

Most presales usually require investors to make big buys. Most have a minimum buy of about $100,000, or about 100 ETH. If you have the funds available, you should definitely buy during the presale. However, many people do not have access to such amounts of money. This does not mean that you cannot get into a presale. The secret is to pool up with other investors and raise the minimum buy amount. The more you raise, the more discounts you will get.

With all the advantages of buying during the presale, you can bet that getting into the presale is going to be a challenge. For ICO's that have generated enough hype, the presale can sell out minutes after being announced. Therefore, if you need to get in at this stage, you should be the very first people who find out about the presale.

Finding out about presales before most other people and determining whether it will become a winner is not an easy task. You need to crawl through tens and hundreds of websites, check out telegram groups, go through slack groups and attend blockchain conferences. This is the only way you can find out about secret ICO's before they are announced.

In case you successfully discover a potential presale that you would like to get into, reach out to the project team explaining why you want to get into the presale and what value you will add to the coin. There are a lot of people who are ready to put huge sums of money into cryptocurrencies, therefore you should aim to provide additional value, other than money. For instance, you can help promote the coin. The best investors are those that can help the project become a success, in addition to providing their money. If you can convince the team that you will add value to the project, you might get the opportunity to participate in the presale.

Chapter Summary

In this chapter, you have learned:

- It's better to invest in ICO's with a long-term view.
- Never invest in a coin if you don't believe in it.
- ICO's that don't reach their hard cap might be hidden gems.
- Always take some profit.
- Make huge investments on promising ICO's and avoid the rest.
- You should take advantage of presales.

In the next chapter, you will learn how to avoid getting scammed.

Chapter Ten: How To Avoid Getting Scammed

In this chapter, you are going to learn about how to avoid losing your money by investing in fake and scam ICO's. You will learn the red flags you need to watch for in order to identify fake ICO's.

Any venture that is capable of turning people into millionaires in the space of a few weeks or months is bound to attract a steady stream of fraudsters and scammers. ICO's are no exception. Owing to the growing popularity of ICO's, the fear of missing out and the overly technical nature of the blockchain ecosystem, many people have found themselves unwittingly putting their money on ICO scams. This is made worse by the fact that some investors contribute money into ICO's without doing any basic research into the ICO. As more and more ICO's hit the market each month, it is becoming increasingly difficult to distinguish genuine ICO's from elaborate scams that dupe investors with flashy names and extensive marketing.

Knowing the red flags to watch out for when evaluating an ICO can protect you from investing your money in projects whose main aim is to separate you from your hard-earned money. Below are some of the things you should watch out for.

An Anonymous Team

One of the most obvious signs of a scam ICO is a project where the team members are anonymous or otherwise unknown. This might seem contradictory when you consider that the identity of Satoshi Nakamoto – Bitcoin's pseudonymous creator – has never been revealed. However, Nakamoto was able to create a successful cryptocurrency because his creation did not have a central authority that users had to place their trust in. On the other hand, by investing in an ICO, you are basically giving your money to the development team and trusting that they will come up with the promised product instead of disappearing with your money.

If the team behind an ICO does not want to be known publicly, there is a high possibility that they might just run away with your money. Others hide their identities because they might have previously committed nefarious acts that they don't want you to find out about.

This does not mean that you should give the green light to any ICO that has listed the team members on its website and whitepaper. Some ICO's go to the extent of creating fake profiles of their supposed team members. Take the time to do your research and ascertain that the members are who they claim to be.

No Clear Use Case

Another red flag that you can use to identify a scam ICO is the failure by the ICO team to articulate a valid use case for the token. For a token to have value, it should serve a key purpose within the ICO's platform. Without such a purpose, it will be impossible for the token to sustain its value. The same case applies for tokens that try to pass themselves as digital currencies without offering any distinct advantages over existing digital currencies.

A good way of determining whether a coin has a real use case is to ask yourself whether the problem it is trying to solve can be solved without using blockchain technology. Not every problem needs blockchain-based solutions and not every system needs to be decentralized. With the current craze around blockchain technology and how it will supposedly disrupt several industries, some people are launching coins to simply ride on this wave. Therefore, if you notice a coin that does not seem to have a real use case, you could be dealing with a scam.

No Clear Roadmap

Any quality ICO will list its development goals, its funding goals, and a clear timeline on how they plan to achieve these goals. If you find that an ICO does not have a clear roadmap, there is a high chance that the ICO team does not have any long-term plans for the project. Instead, they could be driven by the possibility of short-term financial gain. If you find an ICO that has no clear roadmap coupled with a large coin reserve allocated to the ICO team, you should keep away from the ICO.

This does not mean that you should treat any ICO with a roadmap as a legitimate project. Apart from having a roadmap, good ICO's will also have dedicated Telegram and Slack channels where they give potential investors and the public periodic updates on project milestones.

Unrealistic Goals

Sometimes, some ICO's will have a well-articulated use case and a clear roadmap. However, the roadmap might seem to be overly optimistic. If the development schedule seems too optimistic, there is a high chance that the ICO team is being deceptive in a bid to lure more token buyers. Alternatively, they might have set up such an optimistic development schedule because of lack of experience in such projects. Both of these scenarios are not favorable for you as an investor.

Similarly, some ICO's promise enormous returns in a bid to attract investors. A good example of such a scam is PlexCoin, which duped investors into believing that they would see returns of up to 1354% in just 29 days. Common sense dictates that if it sounds too good to be true, it probably is. To avoid falling victim to these unrealistic goals, you should educate yourself on matters related to cryptocurrencies and blockchain technology. You should also conduct due diligence before you decide to put your money into an ICO.

Open-Source Projects With Empty Repositories

If you find that an ICO claims to be an open source project yet it has an empty or non-existent GitHub, there is a very high chance that you are dealing with a scam. One of the main characteristics of most blockchain projects is that they are open source. This means that anyone can access the code, examine it, modify it or redistribute it. Therefore, such projects usually upload their source code to repositories like GitHub. Those with the technical knowledge can then examine the published code and assess the validity and viability of the project. If a project claims to be open source but has not uploaded any files to a public repository, there is a likelihood that the project does not have any actual code.

The Technology

Having files uploaded on public repositories like GitHub should not be taken as a clear indication that the project is legitimate. If you have the technical know-how, download the project code and examine it. If the code appears like a clone of another existing coin, you might be dealing with a scam.

Unfortunately, many people do not have programming experience, therefore examining the project code yourself might be a challenge. However, this does not mean that you cannot gain some insight into the project if you are not a geek. A good way to find some information about the project code is to visit sub-Reddits and other online forums that are dedicated to cryptocurrency and blockchain discussions. Pose your questions to the forum members and watch out for the answers you will receive. Most of the people on these forums are technically savvy, therefore they might offer some great insights into the project.

Mining Structure That Is Skewed To Favor The ICO Team

Sometimes, ICO's make a portion of the coins available to a small group before they are available to the public. This is known as a pre-mine. Sometimes, this is necessary as the pre-mine acts as an incentive to the developers and early investors. However, if you find that a huge portion of the total supply of coins has been reserved for a pre-mine, this should be cause for worry. A development team that favors itself in the allocation of the pre-mine might be looking to maximize its personal financial gain instead of pushing for the long-term success of the project. To determine whether the pre-mine is actually a red flag, you should cross-reference is with the other factors discussed in this chapter.

The Concept

Another good way to find out if the ICO is a scam is to determine if there is a market for whatever the project is proposing. Are there any competitors within that market? How does the new project plan to gain a share of the market? If the ICO has no plan on how it will acquire a share of the market, this should sound some alarm bells. Similarly, you should consider whether there are any traditional solutions to the problem that the blockchain-based project is trying to solve. If there aren't, this is a bad sign. If there are there, does it have a plan on how it will eclipse them?

Compromised Escrow

This is a very important factor in identifying scams. An Escrow is a service that builds trust in transactions by holding funds until certain conditions are met. For instance, let's assume you are buying a certain product from a stranger using Bitcoin. If you send your Bitcoins first, there's a chance that the stranger won't send you the product. If they the product first, you might not send them the Bitcoins. To create trust in this transaction, the Escrow service holds your Bitcoins until you receive the product. Once you receive the product, the Bitcoins are released to the seller. If you do not receive the product, your Bitcoins are returned to you.

ICO's typically have an escrow service that holds investors funds during the ICO. ICO escrows are usually multi-sig wallets. A project member holds one key to the multi-sig wallet while two or more keys are held by trusted members of the community. In such a situation, the project member cannot move the funds without the permission of the other key holders.

In some cases, however, the project members might disguise themselves as one of the trusted community members or a neutral party, in which case they then have the quota needed to move the funds without the permission of the trusted members. A good example of such a scam is the DeClouds scam.

To further reduce the risk of getting scammed, you should look at the kind of escrow being used. Ideally, the escrow should not release all the funds in one go. Instead, the funds should be released in parts once certain developmental milestones are achieved.

Despite the increasing occurrence of ICO scams, you can keep yourself and your money safe by watching out for the red flags discussed in this chapter. Always remember that you should conduct due diligence before investing. You should only contribute your funds to the ICO once you are certain that the ICO is what it claims to be. If it feels or looks like a scam, it is probably a scam. Trust your instincts.

Chapter Summary

In this chapter, you learned:

- Avoid ICO's with anonymous teams.
- Avoid coins without a clear use case.
- Avoid coins with no clear roadmap or unrealistic goals.
- Avoid open source projects that have not uploaded their source code on public repositories.
- Always evaluate the technology behind the coin.
- Avoid coins with a mining structure that is skewed to favor the mining team.
- Avoid ICO's with a compromised escrow.

In the next chapter, you will learn the legal aspects of ICO's.

Chapter Eleven: Legal Aspects of ICO's

In this chapter, we are going to look at the legal stance of the United States and several other countries in relation to ICO's. This will help you determine whether an ICO is bound by financial investment law within your country.

In the last one year, there has been a huge increase in Ethereum-based ICO's, which has in turn led to a new kind of fraud known as pump and dump schemes. These are ICO's where fraudulent teams develop and sell tokens that have no inherent value. These pump and dump schemes have attracted the attention of regulators and securities commissions, whose role is to protect consumers from potentially fraudulent investments. The situation has been made worse by the fact that it is quite challenging to evaluate the legitimacy of a token or to accurately audit an ICO.

As a result of this, and in the absence of any regulations that are specific to ICO's, the US Securities and Exchange

Commission has resorted to categorizing ICO's either as securities or not as a security. Securities are investment possibilities that are traded publicly. These can be created by the issuance of a company's stock through an IPO, through crowd funding or through alternate investment regulations referred to as regulations D, S A+. If an investment opportunity is registered as a security with the SEC, it becomes subject to KYC (Know Your Customer) rules, AML (Anti-Money Laundering) laws and audits. These requirements make it complicated to create and issue ICO's as securities.

To avoid these regulatory issues and the complications they come with, many ICO's have sought to be classified as non-securities. To do this, the ICO's are presenting themselves as new forms of currency that have utility on their respective software platforms. The aim of this is to show that the tokens have a clear value, comparing the tokens to a license to use a software platform. The other route that ICO's can take to avoid being classified as securities is to structure them as donations to non-profit organizations. This way, those who contribute to the ICO are considered to be making donations instead of buying assets that can be traded.

While these approaches provide ways for ICO's to avoid classification as securities, they are not foolproof. The only way to confirm whether an ICO is a security or not is to apply the Howey Test.

What Is The Howey Test And How Does It Apply To ICO's?

The Howey Test is the result of a US Supreme Court case that pitted the SEC against a company known as Howey Co. in 1946. During this case, the Supreme Court came up with a test that could be used to determine whether a transaction constituted an 'investment contract', therefore making it liable to the same laws and regulations that govern securities. Since the SEC vs. Howey Co. court case, the Howey Test has remained the standard test for judging financial instruments in the US.

According to this test, a transaction falls under securities laws and regulations if:

- There is money being invested
- The investment goes to a common enterprise
- The investment is bound to return profits for the investor
- The profits are generated from work done by others other than the investor

When it comes to ICO's, the third point is the most crucial. If an ICO is being promoted as a way to make money, then it is most definitely a security. However, if the tokens to be issued in an ICO are being marketed as pre-orders for a future product without any expected future profits, then the ICO does not fall under securities laws and regulations.

ICO Regulations Internationally

Like the United States, governments around the world are not very certain on how ICO's should be treated. Different countries have different views and approaches.

Singapore

According to the Monetary Authority of Singapore (MAS), holding digital tokens may be taken as a representation of ownership in an asset. Therefore, an ICO could be treated as a collective investment scheme, a share offer, or a debenture, all of which are subject to Singaporean securities laws. This places a legal requirement on the issuers of an ICO to provide a prospectus.

Canada

According to the Canada Securities Administrator (CSA), the coins or tokens sold in a Canadian-based ICO are to be treated as securities in most cases. This requires the economic realities of an ICO to be assessed with the aim of providing protection for investors.

China

Being one of the biggest countries in the cryptocurrency market, it came as a shocker when the People's Bank of

China announced that the country had banned ICO's within the country. So big was the impact of the announcement that is arrested the rise of the price of Bitcoin, something that had seemed unstoppable. With the ban, there is uncertainty over the future of ICO's in the country. However, being the global leader in blockchain technology, there is a high likelihood that the ban will be lifted. However, the resumption of ICO's might come with some attempt at regulations, including requirements for information disclosure and investment risk alerts as well as size limitations on ICO's.

UK

The UK's Financial Conduct Authority has not provided much regulatory guidance on digital currencies, though it has warned consumers that ICO's are *'very high-risk speculative investments'*. This shows that most ICO's in the country are not under the regulation of the FCA. However, companies issuing ICO's in the UK are advised to consider whether their activities fall under the category of services that need to be authorized by the FCA. In addition, the FCA has warned investors to only invest in ICO's if they are confident in the project and if they are experienced in such investments. Since there is no regulation, ICO's present potential for fraud.

Conclusion

While ICO's and cryptocurrencies provide new ways for startups to raise capital and new investment opportunities, they are still in their infancy, which leads to lots of regulatory challenges. Since most operate outside existing regulatory frameworks, not much can be done to ensure investor protection. At the same time, prior to issuing ICO's, companies need to carefully evaluate their activities to determine where their tokens fall and if there are any legal obligations resulting from the same.

Chapter Summary

In this chapter, you have learned:

- How to apply the Howey Test.
- The legal stance on ICO's internationally.

In the next chapter, you will learn the sites where you can keep track of ICO's.

Chapter Twelve: Where To Keep Track of ICO's

In this chapter, you are going to learn about websites where you can keep track of upcoming ICO's. With the increase in the popularity of ICO's, many companies have resulted to issuing ICO's. In 2017, about 2 or 3 ICO's were launched each week. Keeping track of such a huge number of ICO's quickly becomes tasking. To solve this challenge, a number of ICO tracking websites have come up to help investors keep track of all ICO's being planned or launched. Some even provide their own analysis of the ICO's. Below is a list of the most popular ICO tracking lists. If you really want to be up-to-date with everything that happens in the ICO world, I suggest that you join two or three of these sites. One is not enough.

Bitcointalks

Once a company decides to issue an ICO, there is an expectation that the company should issue an ANN, the official announcement of the ICO concept, terms, website and roadmap. Most of these ANNs are done on the Bitcointalk forum. You can keep yourself up to date by following the forum.

Token Market

This is a company that helps companies launch their ICO's. It has feeds which provide news about all upcoming ICO'S. It also has a cryptocurrency exchange. Token Market is a good way of getting notified about high quality ICO's, since most well-known teams have launched their ICO's with the help of Token Market.

Smith + Crown

This is a nice website that keeps a list of upcoming, ongoing and past ICO's. There is a short description of the ICO for each listing. Before listing an ICO on the site, Smith + Crown performs some background research on the ICO company and conducts a live interview with the ICO founders.

Github Ultimate ICO Calendar

Apart from being a popular software development platform, Github is also a great option for keeping track of crowdsourced information. A perfect example of this use is the Github Ultimate ICO Calendar, which compiles information about upcoming and ongoing ICO's, including descriptions about the ICO, launch dates and links to official websites and social media channels.

ICObazaar

This website keeps a list of past, ongoing and upcoming ICO's, together with descriptions of the ICO, explainer videos, founder bios and ICO milestone achievements. It also does an analysis of the investment potential of each listed ICO.

ICO Signal

This site provides a listing of ICO's with short descriptions, launch dates and links to the official ICO websites. However, ICO Signal leans more towards helping ICO companies get word about their ICO out rather than helping investors find the best ICO to invest in.

ICO Stats

This website is more dedicated to past ICO's. While it does list upcoming ICO's, it is best for following the performance of ICO tokens after they are listed in exchanges. It gives detailed data about the price and gives periodic reports on the ROI from these tokens.

Coin-List

This is a site that reviews and publishes information about upcoming and ongoing ICO's after receiving an application. One thing you will like about this site is that it has a great tool that allows you to filter ICO searches by different parameters, including availability of whitepaper, team information, source code and so on.

ICORating

The aim of this website is to rate every ICO. ICORating provides deeply detailed reports on every ICO that is rated on the website. However, this means that ICO's might take some time before being listed on the site since the rating process takes some time.

Coinschedule

This website only provides a list of ongoing and upcoming ICO's. Once an ICO is closed, Coinschedule removes it from the list. The site also has a blog where they post interviews from ICO launchers. Unfortunately, Coinschedule is heavy with ads, which leads to a negative user experience. The site also places ICO's into categories based on industry.

ICOAlert

This is a site that also has a smartphone app that gives you notifications every time a new ICO is launched. The app also gives you notifications once the tokens are listed on an exchange.

ICOCountdown

This site lists upcoming and ongoing ICO's with clocks counting down to the launch or close of the ICO. You will find some ICO's here that are not listed anywhere else. Before listing an ICO, the site performs due diligence to ensure that the ICO is credible.

Crypto Smile

While this website does not have a very huge list of ICO's, it has a nice blog that contains very useful posts about ICO's.

Cyber Fund

This website has a huge list of upcoming ICO's, which are listed by market capitalization. One the ICO closes, it is moved to the market analysis section. Cyber Fund has a six point criteria that they use to determine whether an ICO is fit to be listed on the website.

ICO Tracker

This website provides detailed information about past, ongoing and upcoming token sales. ICO issuers submit their ICO to the site for listing. When an ICO is listed on the site, it is usually accompanied by the name of the person who submitted the ICO for listing and links to the whitepaper and the ICO's social media pages.

ICO List

This website provides a list of closed, open and upcoming ICO's. Each listing is accompanied by the launch and close dates, the ICO targets and the total funds raised for closed ICO's. It also provides detailed information about the ICO, though little verification is done.

Final Words

Thank you for taking the time to read this book.

This book has provided you with a lot of information about ICO's. By now, you know the basics of what ICO's are and how they work, how to value a cryptocurrency and how to evaluate ICO's and pick the right one to invest in. You know how to participate in ICO's and I have also given you the best strategies you can use to make a fortune for yourself with ICO's.

The next step is for you to take the information you have learned from this book and put it to practical use. As with any investment, start small as you learn the ropes. Despite being in their infancy stage, ICO's are a revolutionary way for companies to raise funds, and they are not about to go away any time soon, so take your time and gain practical experience in the markets as you gradually graduate to bigger investments. Once you get the hang of things, there is literally no limit to the amount of money you can make with ICO's.

Finally, I would really appreciate if you take a minute to leave a review for this book. Your feedback is very much appreciated.

I wish you the best luck as you go forward with this new investment opportunity.

www.ingramcontent.com/pod-product-compliance
Lightning Source LLC
Chambersburg PA
CBHW070152230526
45471CB00002B/630